Original title:
Houseplant Haikus

Copyright © 2025 Creative Arts Management OÜ
All rights reserved.

Author: Olivia Sterling
ISBN HARDBACK: 978-1-80581-819-9
ISBN PAPERBACK: 978-1-80581-346-0
ISBN EBOOK: 978-1-80581-819-9

Verdant Vignettes

My leafy friend peeks,
Watching me from the shelf,
Is it me or you,
Whose growth is more absurd?

Patterns of Growth

Curling tendrils laugh,
At my watering routine,
Roots dance through the dirt,
Plea for a little sun.

The Language of Leaves

Each leaf a secret,
Whispers of photosynthesis,
Rolling eyes in shade,
'You missed a day, you know!'

Journey of a Sapling

Tiny sprout in pot,
Dreams of reaching the sky,
But what's that, oh no!
Two weeks without a drink!

Blossoms Beyond the Threshold

Sneaky little sprout,
Eavesdrops on my gossip,
Leaves twitch in delight,
Who knew they cared so much?

Dancing with the dust,
Tiny bugs thrown a rave,
Party starts at dusk,
Nature's own nightlife here.

Lullaby of Leafy Dreams

Whispers in the night,
Plants sing soft melodies,
Ferns sway to the tunes,
Sleepy chlorophyll dreams.

Photosynthesis,
That's how they throw a bash,
Yummy sunlight feast,
And I just watch in awe.

Potted Memories and Joy

Potting soil and laughs,
Spilling secrets like dirt,
Rooted in good times,
Those were the days, my friend.

Bumpy cactus hugs,
Watch your step and your pride,
Needles sharp, but soft,
Best friends from a distance.

Green Resilience in Stillness

Stubborn little leaves,
Defying all the odds,
Still they thrive and laugh,
As I trip on my feet.

Fading light outside,
They say they want a drink,
But it's not their time,
Water my heart instead.

Vases of Vitality

Look at my fern grow,
It's plotting world takeover.
Watch out for the vines,
They whisper leafy lines.

Someone spilled the tea,
Now the pothos drinks with glee.
Tangled in its plan,
A leafy villain, man!

Cultivating Calm

Cactus with a grin,
Pierces hearts with sharpest spin.
Needles are a must,
But still, I'm here to trust.

Basil on the shelf,
A culinary elf.
Chopping makes it dance,
Spices twirl in a trance.

Fronds and Fables

This palm has a joke,
With each sway, it nearly chokes.
Telling tales of sun,
In a breeze, just for fun.

Spider plants conspire,
To create a leafy choir.
Singing 'Never mind!'
They've left their webs behind.

Craving the Rain

Lettuce loves a soak,
Dancing leaves—who needs a cloak?
Raindrops on the soil,
Help us share our toil.

Succulents are wise,
In sun they wear no disguise.
Hiding from the flood,
They chuckle in their mud.

The Poetry of Photosynthesis

Leaves stretch and yawn, hungry for sun,
A slow dance begins, two-step with fun.
Roots sip their tea, roots gossip and laugh,
Chlorophyll dreams of a leafy photograph.

Sunbeams giggle, they tickle the leaves,
Nature's own tease, in shadows it weaves.
Fertilizer jokes, a potent bouquet,
'You're full of yourself!' the plants softly say.

Veils of Verdant Whimsy

Fern fronds flourish, like hair in a breeze,
Wiggly wiggles, they dance to appease.
Cacti in sombreros, what a sight to behold,
Spiny little friends with stories untold.

Petunias pout, in their frilly attire,
'Why wear a hat? We just want to inspire!'
Succulents grin, plump and round,
In the garden's hilarious circus, joy is found.

Echoes Through Green Arches

Ivy climbs high, a green reach for dreams,
Whispers of leaves in the sunlight's beams.
'Who needs a ladder?' the vines will declare,
With a twist and a turn, they float through the air.

Bonsai sits smug, with a wise little nod,
'I'm just a tree, with a very short prod.'
Wobbling pots roll, they couldn't be still,
Green mischief abounds, what a garden thrill!

Finding Calm in the Canopy

Tiny snails picnic, on shady green leaves,
Sipping morning dew, as it gently weaves.
A place of zen, where laughter is soft,
The sound of chill vibes, up high and aloft.

Glaring sun grumbles, 'I'm too hot to play!'
Shade offers refuge, in a leafy ballet.
Nature's embrace, where the silliness thrives,
In a world of great green, oh how fun it thrives!

Longing for Sunshine

My leaves are all drooped,
But the sun is on break,
I'm doing my best,
Could you take a real stake?

Found a cozy spot,
I wedged in a pot,
Guess I'm not too shy,
Just a little hot!

Hello, Mr. Sun,
Can we make a deal?
I'll stretch and I'll twist,
You make me feel real!

A sunburn with flair,
I'll take that all day,
Just find me some light,
I promise to stay!

Roots of Serenity

My roots are all tangled,
In a dance underground,
Just like my thoughts,
When no one's around.

Digging through the dirt,
Feeling quite the mess,
But with all this soil,
I can't help but bless.

Find peace in the grind,
As I grow, oh so slow,
Just give me a shovel,
And watch me steal the show!

Stability's key,
In this life, oh so sweet,
I'll make my own path,
With these little feet!

Breathing in Chlorophyll

Inhales of green air,
Exhales full of zest,
Photosynthesis,
It's all for the best!

Lush greens on my skin,
Sunshine gives me glee,
I see all those rays,
And just want to be free!

Breath of life so fresh,
Crafted with pure love,
If you're feeling down,
Just look to above!

I'm just like a sponge,
Soak up all the glee,
With chlorophyll dreams,
I'm the plant to be!

Shadows in the Soil

Darkness in the earth,
Whispers of the night,
I might seem shy,
But I'm full of light.

Creeping through the gloom,
Roots roam all around,
In this cozy pit,
My laughter resounds.

A shadowy dance,
Like a playful sprite,
I'll sprout up with cheer,
To greet morning light!

So bring on the rain,
And sprinkle with flair,
For in every drop,
I find joy to share!

The Dance of Sunlight and Shade

The sunlight dances,
On leaves that wiggle and sway,
Pot friends chuckle loud,
As shadows play hide and seek.

In corners they beam,
Bright hues of green, life in play,
A spider plant grins,
While ferns do the limbo sway.

Grumpy cacti frown,
Wishing for a bright tan too,
Succulents giggle,
With their plump cheeks aglow.

Life in a small pot,
A party of leafy glee,
Nature's jesters twirl,
In a sunny spotlight jam.

The Echo of Nature in Pots

Whispers in the green,
Tales of soil and sunlight,
A philodendron,
Recounts its wild escapades.

The pothos swings low,
Catch me if you can they tease,
In the quiet room,
Even dirt has witty jokes.

Fiddle leaf fig sighs,
With every stretch and new leaf,
Napping like a pro,
Laughing at those who clutter.

In tiny containers,
Nature's secrets bubble forth,
Chattering with leaves,
A rogue plant throws a party.

Sip of Nature's Essence

Dewdrops on my tongue,
A taste of green, oh so fresh,
Mint sprigs laugh with joy,
As I pluck them for my tea.

A basil's wink so sly,
Season my life with humor,
Thyme joins the joke,
Kneading laughter into bread.

Herbs in the kitchen,
Taking over all the space,
Time for a squeeze now,
Basil's feeling quite saucy.

A sip of green bliss,
In every herbal concept,
Nature's light-hearted,
Creating joy in every brew.

The Silent Growth of Green

In the corner they sit,
Cacti plotting world takeovers,
While I just water,
Thinking I'm the boss here.

Leaves whisper secrets,
Unbeknownst to my keen ears,
That their next big plan,
Involves my shoe collection.

Watching them thrive here,
Do they have a hidden goal?
To utterly mock,
My gardening skills, such glee!

Each sprout a rebel,
Defying all my control,
Yet, I can't help but,
Love their leafy attitudes.

Leaf Fragments on the Window Sill

Little green confetti,
Fallen from a dancing leaf,
Now the cats feast here,
With a crunchy delight.

Sunlight sneaks between,
The glass panes in my old home,
It spotlights the mess,
Like art in a gallery.

Dust bunnies join in,
A party no one invited,
Nature's own ballet,
Both messy and a delight.

Every leaf that drops,
Tells a story, gives a laugh,
While I sip my tea,
Munching on my own snacks.

Fern Fronds and Gentle Breezes

Whisking through the ferns,
Their fronds wave as if to say,
Twirling in the breeze,
Life is too short, join the fun.

I case a shadow,
A spider spins its grand web,
While I dance around,
Calling myself the gardener.

In this wild forest,
Pleather boots and all, I strut,
Pretending to know,
What secret plants can whisper.

Giggles fill the air,
Pests play hide-and-seek with me,
Oh little green friends,
You're the joy I didn't see.

Urban Jungle on a Shelf

A jungle of chaos,
Plants jostling for living space,
While I just watch calm,
My heart racing with each sprout.

Tiny pots hold dreams,
Succulents yodel out loud,
Telling tales of life,
In their perfect little worlds.

In my concrete maze,
They thrive and then sometimes wilt,
A quirky meltdown,
Just like my daily coffee.

Shelf looks like my mind,
Total clutter, yet some peace,
Who needs vacation?
When you've got greens in the sun.

Heartbeats in Clay

In pots they reside,
Chasing sunlight all day,
I water with care,
They pretend to be okay.

Tiny leaves start to shake,
Like they're in a dance,
Soaking up all the rays,
While I just take a glance.

Green Companions in Sunlight

My plants have the glow,
They gossip, oh so sly,
'Is that a new leaf sprout?'
Or 'Check out that fly!'

With each tiny bloom,
I throw them a feast,
But when I say 'dinner',
They say 'We prefer yeast!'

Whispering Leaves at Dawn

Each morning they speak,
With secrets so profound,
'Water me now, please!'
As I stretch on the ground.

They know my routine,
But rarely behave,
Spilling dirt on the floor,
Just to misbehave.

Beneath the Leafy Canopy

Underneath their shade,
I ponder my next meal,
They stare with envy,
While I just want to squeal.

They laugh at my jokes,
(If they only could talk),
But their quiet green smiles,
Make me feel like a rock.

Sunlit Corners and Nature's Grace

In sunlit corners,
A cactus dreams of rain.
Who needs a shower?
Just bask in bright rays.

Ferns plot world domination,
As dust bunnies conspire.
They giggle in whispers,
With dirt on their hands.

The succulents snicker,
'We don't need much water!'
Our roots are so clever,
We'll thrive on neglect.

Lettuce traipses around,
In its salad disguise.
Twirling with laughter,
At the sight of carrots.

Harmony in Hanging Vines

Vines swing in the breeze,
Having a grand old time.
They climb right over me,
Thinking they own the place.

Spider plants are watchful,
With eyes big and twinkly.
They gossip in green,
About the pot next door.

Pothos curls and laughs,
'Think you can outgrow me?'
But I'm a warrior,
I'll twist and I'll turn!

I'm always just hanging,
Not a care in the world.
When life gives you vines,
You dance with the fun!

The Tender Care of Green

Water drops like kisses,
On leaves that love to shine.
They glisten and giggle,
'Oh, what a life we lead!'

Soil gives a soft chuckle,
As roots stretch and wiggle.
'Plant me a nice dinner,
Of worms and some rain!'

Sunbeams come to play,
With shadows that tickle.
Each leaf a little dancer,
In green ballet shoes.

A whisper of breeze,
Plays tag with all the leaves.
'Tender care and light,
We're a family here!'

Soft Touch of Nature Indoors

A tiny green sprout,
Poking through the old pot.
'What's the fuss about?
Just give me some sun!'

Dust settles like snow,
On the shelf of good thoughts.
Plants giggle and cheer,
'Time to do our dance!'

My rubber tree's strict,
On all its care instructions.
But leaf after leaf,
It pushes for hugs.

In this little space,
Nature gives a warm wink.
With laughter and joy,
Moving in for a cuddle.

The Poetry of Petals

In the sun, I sway,
Telling stories of dust,
Blades of grass listen,
Green poets, no fuss.

My blooms burst with laughter,
A raucous parade,
I whisper sweet secrets,
To the bees, unafraid.

Sunburnt leaves grumble,
"Too much bright!" they scold,
I giggle and bask,
In glories of gold.

With morning dew's kiss,
I open my eyes,
A cheerful salute,
To the brightening skies.

Impressions in a Leaf

A speck on my leaf,
A bug's tiny picnic,
Cucumbers, please stay,
Don't make me a lick!

Sipping on sunlight,
My cocktail divine,
Watch me grow taller,
While you stay benign.

Overwatered friend,
Such a dramatic tale,
"Float me a rescue!"
No need to turn pale.

Gazing at my pot,
Dreams of wild places,
With legs like a sprout,
In soft, leafy spaces.

Tranquil Moments in Green

I brew sleepy vibes,
With leaves all a-quiver,
Drifting in stillness,
A plant's chill river.

When the cat leaps high,
Like a ninja in green,
I hold my breath tight,
In this leafy scene.

Moss hopes for a hug,
While ferns strike a pose,
Together we laugh,
At the chaos that grows.

With roots in the dirt,
I meditate slow,
In my pot, zen bliss,
As the breezes blow.

Secrets of the Succulent Soul

In a pot so snug,
A secret I keep,
Drink water like tea,
But don't lose your sleep.

Cacti wear armor,
Yet, they long for a mate,
They prick up their spines,
On love, they debate.

Pearly beads of joy,
Shimmer on my skin,
I bask in the warmth,
Let the fun begin!

With each tiny bloom,
I send out a cheer,
A succulent party,
Come join, never fear!

Petals of Peace

In sunlit corners,
My leafy friend stands tall,
Shades of green abound,
Whispers of calm greet all.

Potted in a bowl,
It seems to mock my care,
Drink up, then droop low,
Oh, the drama we share.

Tiny bugs parade,
Like they own my space, too,
With a mischievous smile,
They enjoy the view.

Yet with all this fun,
I still chat every day,
These buds bring such joy,
In their quirky way.

Growth in the Quiet Space

In the quiet room,
A cactus holds its stance,
Prickly but so proud,
It's a spiky romance.

In shadows it waits,
Water's a rare delight,
A sip then a slump,
Oh, what a funny sight.

Leaves in all the wrong,
Colors that make me guess,
When did you turn blue?
Nature's own game of chess.

The fern is a diva,
Fanning for attention,
I laugh at its moves,
What a grand invention!

A Symphony of Sprouts

Dancing in their pots,
With roots bound tight below,
They sway to my tunes,
In a concert no one knows.

Peppers with a wink,
Tomatoes blush with pride,
Basil's sassy flair,
In this crazy green ride.

Each sprout has a voice,
Though soft and with a cheer,
When I hum along,
They giggle, I can hear.

Nature's steadfast gang,
Growing wild as they play,
In this tiny farm,
We keep boredom away.

Nature's Touch in Tiny Pots

In pots lined in rows,
Life thrives in hues so bright,
A cast of misfits,
Under the soft moonlight.

Little ferns wiggle,
While succulents look smug,
They laugh at my skill,
Which fails with every snug.

Sometimes they will droop,
As if holding a grudge,
'Water me today'
Before I go on judge.

Yet these goofy greens,
Colour my day with glee,
In this jungle small,
Nature's comedy.

Mesmerizing Mists around the Foliage

I spritz and I spray,
Tiny jungle dance begins,
My leaves drink from the sky,
While I wonder, who's on spin?

A misty shower glow,
Ferns twirl swaying with delight,
My cat joins the show,
As plants whisper, "Who's a fright?"

Bamboo laughs so tall,
A cactus grins in its spikes,
In this funny hall,
We share secrets and likes.

The orchids tease me,
"Give us sunlight! Not your woes!"
I chuckle with glee,
Plants and I, all in our throes.

A Symphony of Freshness

In harmony blooms,
A chorus of green delight,
Succulents in tune,
While I tap my feet just right.

A leaf, a backbeat,
My herbs hum a jazzy twist,
Each sprout feels the heat,
While I try not to assist.

Fiddle leaf so proud,
Cactus strums a prickly song,
Nature's little crowd,
Where the laughter feels so strong.

Yet my watering can,
Hits a note that spills away,
Plants laugh as they can,
"Join the garden ballet today!"

The Art of Indoor Eden

In my little nook,
A jungle of giggly greens,
Plants tell me to look,
At my life's botanical scenes.

Painted leaf charades,
In pots, absurdist portraits,
Stems in silly parades,
Nature's cleverest traits.

My dracaena spins,
As if it won a grand prize,
In the house of sins,
Where all decorum flies.

A mischievous vine,
Giggles as it climbs so high,
Chasing light, it's fine,
While I just sit and sigh.

Among the Botanical Spirits

In whispers we meet,
Among leafy spirits bright,
Conversations sweet,
Floating in the morning light.

The pothos giggles,
Making shadows dance and sway,
While I keep still,
And struggle to find my way.

My spider plant weaves,
Tales of the garden's old paths,
While I try to breathe,
Laughter ending in soft laughs.

An agave served wine,
In that pot, oh, it's divine!
"Best party of the year!"
Said the flora, bright and clear.

Foliage Dreams

Green on the window,
Reaching for sunlight,
Chasing my shadow,
Dancing in delight.

Forgotten water,
But look how I thrive!
Dust bunny friends join,
In this leafy hive.

A pot of secrets,
Napping in the sun,
Whispering to leaves,
'We're in this for fun!'

A spider friend crawls,
With legs that amuse,
'Don't eat my greens now,
Or others will lose!'

Thriving in Silence

Quietly I bloom,
In a world so loud,
Happy to just be,
In my little crowd.

Dust storms around me,
Yet I stand quite tall,
Sip from my own cup,
Ignoring it all.

I watch the humans,
As they rush about,
I just shake my leaves,
And laugh without doubt.

In stillness, I grow,
With roots intertwined,
In their busy lives,
My joy they can't find.

Oasis in a Room

Under a soft light,
I'm a jungle in here,
Leafy green haven,
Where I shed all fear.

I'm a vacation,
In an office space,
With no plane ticket,
Just a leaf's embrace.

Humans walk by me,
With worries in tow,
I can't help but grin,
To see their woe grow.

Sip your coffee fast,
While I soak the sun,
In this tiny world,
We both can have fun.

Curled Ferns and Open Hearts

Curled ferns whisper,
Secrets of the morn,
With hearts wide open,
Not a worry born.

I stretch out my fronds,
In eager delight,
Keep your worries, friend,
I'm your soothing sight.

When the day gets tough,
You can count on me,
To offer a smile,
And a leafy spree.

With the sun shining,
And potting soil here,
Let's laugh at the world,
With a cup of cheer.

A Symphony of Green

In the corner, she tries,
A cactus with spiky pride.
Music? Just a hum, friend.
Be careful, or you'll get poked.

Dance of leaves in sunlight,
Ferns sway with a gentle grace.
But watch out for the cat,
He thinks they're his new foes.

Succulent in a crown,
Hoping for a royal feast.
Salad is not on menu,
But green is still the dream.

Bonsai with tiny dreams,
Planning world domination.
Yet stuck in this small pot,
His throne, a ceramic mess.

Potted Poetry

A leafy being sighs,
I'm bored of just standing here.
Do you think I could dance?
Perhaps when the sun comes out.

Moss on the window sill,
Whispers secrets of the day.
'Kiss me, I'm so thirsty!'
But the glass is way too far.

In my tiny pot home,
I contemplate my next move.
Should I reach for sunlight?
Or just nap until it shines?

Each day I stretch and flex,
Exercising like a champ.
But who gets the last laugh?
No abs, just a lovely leaf.

Echoes of Springtime

When spring wakes me up,
I shake off the winter blues.
Fresh buds start to bloom,
Nothing like a new debut.

Bees come buzzing near,
Roses flaunt their lovely hues.
But I'm just a leaf,
Wishing I could fly with them.

Friends in pots nearby,
They gossip 'bout the weather.
A sage with a smirk says,
'Just grow tall and stay chill, man.'

We toast with our roots,
A party underground ledge.
Though soil gets quite dusty,
It's fun down here, I swear!

Sips of Dew

Morning mist arrives,
A gentle sip on my leaves.
Oh, how refreshing!
I'll take another, please.

Dew drops dance and sway,
Like tiny pearls of laughter.
But wait, what's that sound?
The cat's plotting my downfall!

Each sip of coolness,
Reminds me of sunny days.
But storms bring such thrills,
As I sway with wild delight.

Underneath the sun,
I'm a proud little green star.
With every giggle,
Nature's comedy unfolds.

A Garden in a Whisper

In the corner light,
A cactus holds a secret,
Spiking all the fun,
No one dares to cuddle.

Pothos climbs the shelf,
While succulents have gossip,
'We're low maintenance',
But watch me steal sunlight!

Fern waves with style,
In its busy green jacket,
'Why am I so cool?'
It knows how to relax.

Spider plant chuckles,
When dust bunnies get too close,
'You call that my meal?'
It's a feast for the brave.

Leaves of Serenity

In morning's soft light,
A peace lily whispers low,
'Please don't drown me, friend!'
I promise I'll bloom bright.

Fiddle leaf takes pride,
'Look I'm taller than the door!'
But with each new leaf,
It bends in a shy bow.

Calathea sways slow,
Patiently telling a tale,
Of the rainy days,
When it danced like no one cared.

Zamioculcas grins wide,
'I'm tough, but soft on the inside,'
Frowning when it drinks too,
'Less water, more sunshine!'

The Coziness of Green

In a blanket's fold,
The aloe's tucked in just right,
'Come, let's binge-watch shows,
I'm soothing and snappy, too.'

Dust on the window,
The peace lily gave a sigh,
'If I had a hand,
I'd dust myself off, you know.'

Where the sunlight beams,
The snake plant stands at attention,
'You might call me sharp,
But I'm a friend with long roots.'

Tiny pots in rows,
Each with tales they want to share,
Who'll spill the first tea?
The laughter echoes greenly.

Leafy Conversations

Monstera waves high,
'Why do they call me Swiss cheese?'
'Because of your holes,'
Said the lilting philodendron.

Dracaena rolls eyes,
'You think you're the coolest here,'
While Aloe just nods,
'We're all part of this fun team!'

The room fills with joy,
As sunlight fills the corners,
'Let's throw a dance-off,
In honor of growth and shade!'

Laughing as they grow,
A world of green giggles loud,
'One more droplet, please,
Let's splash in the morning dew!'

Seasons in a Ceramic Bowl

In spring, leaves giggle,
Sunshine whispers secrets,
Pot feels like a stage,
Buds bloom with big dreams.

Summer's a leafy rave,
Dancing in the warm gust,
Soil splashes on my pants,
Why is dirt so funny?

Autumn sees things change,
Falling leaves like confetti,
Pots now gather dust,
Where did all the green go?

Winter's a sleepy tale,
Potted friends shiver softly,
I swear they rolled their eyes,
Snow? Let's stay indoors, folks!

Dance of the Potted Plants

Potatoes in a pot,
Twirling like wild foodies,
Tomatoes sing a tune,
Lettuce rolls its own way.

Cacti do the limbo,
Needles sharp, humor too,
Succulents sway gently,
Just don't poke the bear!

Herbs hum a little jig,
Basil spins, and thyme twirls,
Mint drops a beat, yo,
Salsa in the window!

Fern flirts with sunlight,
Wiggling, waving hello,
I join their dance crew,
Can you see my moves too?

Mirror of the Garden's Heart

Sunlight checks its makeup,
Reflects off leafy crowns,
A silky green smile,
Then all the plants just blush.

Butterflies gossip here,
Chatting about flower styles,
"Your petals are fab!"
"Yours? So 'blooming' bright!"

Grass whispers soft secrets,
"Do you think roots can hear?"
Frogs croak the answer,
While worms roll their approval.

Bees buzz round in circles,
Humming tunes of sweet life,
Plants nod with big dreams,
In their mirror of joy!

Essence of Evergreen Serenity

Pine sits and breathes deep,
Says, "Relax, it's a breeze!"
Needles fall like laughter,
Nature's ticklish prank!

Spruce tries new yoga poses,
Stretching to reach the sky,
Evergreen philosophies,
"Breathe, let things just grow."

Cedar tells old wise tales,
Filled with knots and knowledge,
"Branches hold the past gently,
Embrace the bends of life!"

In this plant-filled room,
Serenity brews softly,
Smiles bloom all around,
It's quite a leafy show!

Interludes of Ivy

In the corner, I sway,
Green fingers tickle the wall.
Just another day here,
As I prepare to enthrall.

Dust my leaves, they insist,
But I thrive on neglect.
Whispering secrets to air,
I'm the plant you respect.

Sunbathing is my game,
With a bright, goofy grin.
Catch me stretching in light,
I'm a true leafy win.

Sometimes I lose a leaf,
Oops, there goes my new clout!
I'll just grow a new one,
That's what I'm all about!

Soft Succulence in a Sunbeam

In the sunlight I bask,
Plump with laughter and joy.
Watch the humans tiptoe,
Around their little ploy.

Shiny and round, I sit,
Filling up with delight.
"Don't touch!" they scream in fear,
I'm a prickly insight.

I listen closely at night,
To gossip of the moon.
All about those thunderheads,
That bring birds out of tune.

When they forget to water,
I flourish with dry pride.
"Succulent and sassy!"
I laugh while they decide.

Kaleidoscope of Botanical Bliss

Colors dance on my leaves,
A party just for me.
Here's the thing, dear friend—
I'm a polka-dot spree.

Watch those stripes swirl and spin,
While the cats make a mess.
I'm the art on this shelf,
Chaos in leafy dress.

Tiny bugs find it fun,
To prance upon my veins.
I'll host their little dance,
And drink through their refrains.

As the day slips away,
I shimmer in delight.
A prism in a pot,
Stars twinkling goodnight!

Earth's Breath in Indoor Spaces

I'm the quietest guest,
But I love a good laugh.
Each tick of the clock, I bloom,
A jester in green half.

Neighbor cats eye with glee,
"Oh, a nibble!" they plot.
Little do they all know,
I'm a seasoned old bot.

Snakes and succulents thrive,
They slink in vibrant glee.
We gossip of the sun,
While sipping on soft tea.

When humans stroll on by,
I wave with a plant wink.
"Oh, don't mind me, dear friend,
It's just my indoor schtick!

Serenity in Succulents

In a pot so small,
A cactus won't hug back,
Prickly conversations,
Such a one-sided knack.

Succulents stand so proud,
With leaves that love the sun,
Tell me your secret,
How to be this fun!

Water me just a sip,
But not an entire sea,
I promise not to droop,
Just show some sympathy.

Potty humor galore,
I'm feeling pretty spry,
As long as I stay green,
You can't let me die!

Growing Within Walls

In corners I hide,
Growing vines that creep slow,
Wish I could roam free,
But walls say, 'No, no!'

I stretch toward the light,
A lanky little dude,
Hoping for some space,
Or some plant food mood.

You prune me back like hair,
But I just won't quit,
A rebellious sprout,
Not a lazy old twit!

Every speck of dust,
Is a feast, I declare,
A little gourmet,
Crispy snacks everywhere!

Nature's Gentle Embrace

Leaves tickle my skin,
Nature's fun little game,
Sunshine on my face,
I'm feeling no shame!

I sway in the breeze,
A dance with a slight twist,
My pot spins around,
Nature, don't be missed!

A ladybug lands,
Living rent-free right here,
I charge her no fees,
Though I'm still a bit queer.

With soil on my toes,
I laugh at every pest,
Funny how they think,
They'll take my leafy zest!

Tending to Tranquility

Woke up bright and fresh,
With coffee in my hand,
But my fern's a mess,
Time for a caring plan.

I trim the wild fronds,
And talk like they can hear,
My plants think I'm mad,
But they're the ones so dear!

Each morning's a chore,
In joy, I sing a tune,
If they could just laugh,
We'd sway beneath the moon.

A zany little crew,
With potting soil galore,
We'll plant jokes all day,
And keep wanting more!

Lush Life in Every Corner

Green leaves like umbrellas,
Hiding snacks from my cat.
She plots her next attack,
While I water the plants.

Cactus on the windowsill,
No hugs, it gives a poke.
But it's the best listener,
No need for a joke!

Sprouts peeking out with glee,
"Am I a tree today?"
Each pot has its quirks,
Sunny side for display!

Those tiny pots all smug,
Saying, "We're all that's fun!"
Little jungle party,
But I'm the only one!

Breath of Chlorophyll

Feeling green, oh what fun,
My fern twirls under sun.
It whispers jokes to me,
"Do you think I'm overrun?"

The neighbor's plant's a diva,
Always demanding light.
I just roll my eyes hard,
And give it a good fright.

Basil dreams of pasta days,
Mint wants a band to play.
They're all just silly buds,
Life's flavors on display!

I talk to my peonies,
They nod 'cause they're quite wise.
No need for a therapist,
Just watch them in disguise.

In the Comfort of Clay

A pot of mischief waits,
Hiding secrets so deep.
My succulents snicker soft,
As they gather and peep.

Soil spills across the floor,
"Oops," says the shyest sprout.
I laugh, it's good to know,
Even plants can freak out!

Each morning brings new quirks,
Lettuce plays hide and seek.
Who knew greens had such sass?
Veggies? They're quite unique!

But as the day draws in,
Leaf shadows start to dance.
In this crowd of green friends,
I take my silly chance.

Roots Entwined with Wonder

The roots are all gossiping,
Under the soil they scheme.
"Did you hear the news?" shouts one,
"Fertilizer's a dream!"

Little leaves sway in tune,
"Let's throw a planty bash!"
The pots all shake and hum,
Until one makes a crash.

"Was that a sunny joke?"
They giggle and they play.
We're all just potted pals,
Living in mossy sway!

Time ticks for greens and blooms,
Growing tall is the goal.
In this leafy circus,
Every day's a new role.

www.ingramcontent.com/pod-product-compliance
Lightning Source LLC
Chambersburg PA
CBHW070333120526
44590CB00017B/2864